TIMELESS TALES

Tales of Wonder

Retold by TANA REIFF

Illustrated by HOLLY J. DOBBS

NEW READERS PRESS

Library of Congress Cataloging-in-Publication Data

Reiff, Tana.
Tales of wonder / retold by Tana Reiff ;
illustrated by Holly J. Dobbs.
p. cm. — (Timeless tales)
Summary: Ten folktales from around the world,
including "Why the Sea Is Salty," and "The Firebird."
ISBN 0-88336-459-X
1. Readers for new literates. 2. Fantastic fiction.
[1. Folklore.] I. Dobbs, Holly J., ill. II. Title. III. Series:
Reiff, Tana. Timeless tales.
PE1126.A4R446   1993
428.6'2—dc20   93-16083
                                  CIP
                                  AC

Contents

Introduction

A tale of wonder is like a good dream—it's not real, but it's fun. You get to visit some very different places where strange things happen.

The tales in this book visit magic gardens, fly to heaven, and travel to the end of the world. You'll read about a bird that looks like fire, an elephant that flies, and animals that talk. People in these stories make wishes. A mill grinds out anything at all. A plant makes a sick person well. Water makes old people young.

Some tales of wonder teach a lesson. In "The Three Wishes," "The Elephant from Heaven," "The Fountain of Youth," and "Why the Sea Is Salty," people find out what happens when they want too much. In "A Strange Place to Visit," a young man learns why all play and no work isn't good. In "The Thunderbird," a giant pays a price for being selfish. "The Firebird" and "The Magic Eagle" are about people who go through plenty of adventure to get what they want.

Some of the stories are just plain fun. In "The Mirror," people think there is magic even when there isn't. In "Talk," it's not a person who gets "the last word."

Sometimes a tale of wonder can tell us something true about real life. Other times we can forget real life, while the story lets us dream. Either way, we seem to need our stories. That is why we keep them for so long.

The Firebird*

Russia

"Someone is taking apples from my beautiful golden apple tree!" the old tsar (ZAR)** told his son, Ivan. "Every morning when I visit my garden, another apple is gone. Seven apples have been taken already!"

"I will find out who is doing this," Ivan said.

That night young Ivan sat under the golden apple tree. He waited for someone to show up, and almost went to sleep. Then, all of a sudden, the garden was filled with a bright light. Ivan heard the sound of wings. There before him was a large, beautiful bird. Her feathers were so golden that she looked like flying fire. The firebird landed in the tsar's apple tree.

---

*This is one version of many Russian legends about a "firebird."

**A tsar, or czar, was like a king in old Russia.

Just as the firebird reached for an apple, Ivan grabbed her by the tail. But the firebird got away, and Ivan was left holding nothing but one golden feather. When morning came, Ivan went to show it to his father.

"I am glad we know who has been taking my golden apples," the tsar said to Ivan. "Now I want you to bring me the whole bird."

Ivan set out on the tsar's best horse. He rode for weeks. One day he stopped at a field. As soon as Ivan got off the horse, it turned to stone. Then he saw a large wolf looking him up and down.

"This is my field," the wolf said to Ivan. "Go away, or I will turn you to stone, too."

"I am looking for the firebird," said Ivan.

"I see," the wolf said. "In that case, hop on my back. I will take you to the firebird. She is at the end of the world."

The wolf ran faster than any horse. In no time at all, Ivan was at the end of the world.

"Behind this wall lives an evil wizard," said the wolf, pointing to a stone wall. "The firebird belongs to him. He sends her to your father's garden to steal the golden apples."

Ivan looked over at the wall. It was very high.

"Climb that wall," the wolf said. "On the other side is the wizard's garden. There you will find the firebird in a cage. Reach in and take her. Do not touch the cage, or the wizard's men will come after you."

Ivan did as the wolf said. But when he saw the firebird, he wasn't sure he could hold on to her. So he picked up the whole cage. As soon as he did that, the wizard's men jumped out of the bushes. They tied up Ivan with ropes and dragged him into a horse barn.

When the wizard's men left Ivan, the wolf came into the barn.

"I told you not to touch the cage," the wolf said. He chewed the rope until it broke, and Ivan was free. "Next time maybe you will listen."

As Ivan and the wolf were leaving the barn, Ivan spotted a beautiful horse. It was as white as milk, with a golden tail. "Look at that horse!" Ivan said.

"The wizard also took that horse," the wolf explained. "It belongs to a young queen named Irena. The wizard keeps her in his tower."

"I must save both Irena and her horse," said Ivan.

"I will help you," said the wolf. "But you must wait until everyone is asleep. And you must touch only what you go to get."

Late that night, Ivan went back into the wizard's garden. He took only the firebird. The wolf kept the bird while Ivan climbed the tower and slipped into Irena's window.

There, beside the sleeping queen's bed, were the tsar's seven golden apples. "The evil wizard must have wanted the apples to please this young woman," Ivan said to himself. "I can't leave my father's apples behind." So he put them in his pockets. Then he lifted up the sleeping queen. As he looked at her face, he couldn't believe how lovely she was. He held her carefully and climbed back down the tower.

Ivan carried the sleeping queen into the barn. He climbed up on her white horse with the golden tail. The wolf waited outside with the firebird on his back. Then they all headed down the road toward home.

"What is in your pockets?" the wolf called to Ivan.

"I got my father's apples back!" Ivan called back.

"I told you to touch only what you went to get!" said the wolf.

Just then Ivan heard the sound of another horse. He looked back. The evil wizard himself was riding fast behind them.

Ivan reached into his pocket for an apple. He threw it at the wizard, but the wizard caught it  and put it inside his shirt. Ivan threw another apple and another. The wizard caught six in a row.

Then Ivan threw the last golden apple. It hit the evil wizard on the head, and he fell to the ground. Ivan jumped off his horse and pulled the apples out of the wizard's shirt.

Just then the firebird began
to sing. Irena woke up when
she heard its lovely song.
"Where am I?" she asked.

Ivan told her everything that had happened.
"You are safe now," he promised her.

Irena was very happy to see her
white horse. "You are good to save
my horse and me," she said. "And the
firebird will be your friend now that
she is free. Thank you, Ivan."

Ivan, Irena, the wolf, and the firebird went
on their way. When they reached the wolf's
field, the wolf said, "You won't need me
anymore. I will stay here."

There in the field stood Ivan's horse, which
had turned to stone. The wolf brought the
horse back to life and Ivan jumped on its back.
Irena rode her own horse.

During the last part of the trip, Ivan asked
Irena to marry him. She said yes.

When the tsar saw that Ivan had brought
him the firebird, he was pleased beyond words.
He gave Ivan and Irena a big wedding. The
firebird stayed in the tsar's garden. She flew
free, never in a cage. And she never again took
a golden apple.

The Three Wishes

Puerto Rico and Other Places

 A woodcutter and his wife lived in the woods. They were as poor as they could be. Yet they were happy because they loved each other and always shared with others.

Every day the husband went out to cut wood. His wife stayed home alone doing her own work. One day a little old man came to the door.

"Please, dear woman, have you something for a poor man to eat?" he begged.

"There is never much food in this house," said the woman. "However, I would be happy to share these beans with you."

The little old man ate every last bean. Then he said, "You are very kind. For giving me these beans, I will give you three wishes. Think of what you want. These things will be yours."

"Oh, my!" said the wife. "I wish my husband could be here now!"

As soon as the words left her mouth, her husband was standing before her. "What am I doing here?" he asked, looking very surprised.

The wife hugged her husband. "This sweet old man gave me three wishes. Isn't that nice? I was wishing that you could be here and, sure enough, here you are!"

But the woodcutter was angry. "Don't you see?" he said. "You wasted a wish. You could have wished for any number of things that we need. Now we have only two wishes left. You are so stupid! May you grow donkey ears!"

As soon as the words left his mouth, his wife's ears grew large, long, and furry.

13

"Look what you've done!" she cried. "You wished for me to grow donkey ears, and I did. Now we have only one wish left. What shall we wish for?"

"Perhaps you want money?" asked the little old man. "Perhaps power? Name it and it will be yours."

"We were happy before we had three wishes," said the woodcutter. "We got along fine until now. I wish we could be as we were before."

As soon as the words left his mouth, his wife's donkey ears were gone.

"Your third wish has come true," said the little old man. "You see, having what you wish for cannot always make you happy. Because you now understand this, I will give you a very special gift."

With that, he left the woodcutter and his wife alone. He did not say what the gift would be. But the next year, the gift came. It was a child. The family was still poor. But they were as happy as they could be.

The Fountain of Youth

Japan

Once upon a time, an old man walked along a river bank on a very hot day. Needing a drink of water, he bent down by a pool in the river. He cupped his hands and drank the clear water. In all his years, he had never tasted water like this. It was clean and sweet, but a bit strange. "I hope it's all right," he said to himself.

Just then he saw a face in the water. He knew this face, yet he didn't. Who could it be? Then the man knew the face was his. But he looked as he had when he was a very young man.

15

"I have found the Fountain of Youth!" he cried.

The man ran home to tell his wife the news. "Who are you?" the old woman asked when he walked into the house.

"I am your husband!" said the man. "I have found the Fountain of Youth! I am young again!"

"I too must drink that water," said the old woman. "A young man like you won't want a wife as old as I am."

Her husband told her where to find the magic pool. Off went the old woman to find it.

When she found the pool, she took a long, cool drink of water. Then she took another. And another. With each drink she became younger.

Her husband waited for his wife to return. After a few hours, he began to worry. So he set off for the river.

You see, it is possible to drink too much water from the Fountain of Youth. That is what the wife had done. By the time her husband found her, she had become a baby again. There on the river bank she lay on her little back, kicking her legs and crying for all the world to hear.

The Elephant from Heaven

India and Pakistan

Once there was a man named Kanai. His favorite thing to do was to keep a fine garden. He grew flowers and fruit trees of all sorts. Everything Kanai grew was the best of its kind.

One day, as Kanai was working in his garden, a strong wind began to blow. It felt like a storm coming. The flowers bent to the ground, and the young fruit trees blew until they broke.

Kanai covered his head with his hands and ran for cover. But as he ran, he looked toward the sky. Then he knew that this was not really a storm. What he saw was a large elephant flying toward Earth. On its legs were gold bands. On its head was a fancy hat. Shiny ribbons were tied around the elephant's tusks.

Never in his life had Kanai seen an elephant like this! Surely, it must be from heaven.

The elephant landed in the garden. It stepped on the flowers. It ate Kanai's fruit. It tore out some big trees. Then it began to fly away. Kanai decided to go along. He grabbed the elephant's little tail, and the two of them went up toward heaven.

When the elephant landed in heaven, Kanai looked all around. Everything was more wonderful than he had ever dreamed. There were fine, large houses, streets of gold, and the best bazaar* that ever could be. The fruits in the bazaar were even better than those Kanai grew

---

Bazaar is the Arabic word for street market.

on Earth. And the jewels! They were so big and cost so little. Kanai just had to buy one for his wife, Kali.

When Kanai had finished shopping, he waited for the elephant's next trip to Earth. Once again he grabbed the elephant's tail and tagged along.

"Where have you been?" asked Kali when Kanai got home.

Kanai showed her the jewel. "I've been to heaven," he said. "Look what I bought you at the bazaar! Everything there cost very little money!"

"You went to heaven and back?" asked Kali. "I want to go, too. When can I go?"

"Next time the elephant flies down to our garden," said Kanai. "But please don't tell anyone. We don't want this to get around. People might think we are crazy."

The next day Kali ran into her best friend. She could not keep the secret. "I'm going for a ride to heaven!" Kali said. "They sell big jewels up there for very little money. But please don't tell anyone."

Kali's friend couldn't keep the secret either. She told her husband. He told his best friend. That person told someone else.

Before long a whole crowd of people showed up at Kanai's garden. Everyone waited for the elephant from heaven. Everyone wanted the good buys at the bazaar in the sky.

Kanai wasn't happy that so many people knew the secret. But now that they were there, they might as well go along.

"Here's how we'll do it," Kanai began. "I will grab the elephant's tail. Kali will hold on to my feet. Her best friend will hold on to Kali's feet. And so on. Does everyone understand?"

"Yes, yes," everyone said.

Just then the elephant landed. Kanai grabbed its tail and everyone held on behind him. Up they all went into the sky, one after another, like a chain.

As they flew, Kali's friend asked her, "Just how big was that jewel, anyway?"

"Kanai," called Kali to her husband. "Tell my friend how big that jewel was."

"About this big," said Kanai as he spread his arms wide apart.

What a mistake! Kanai
had let go of the elephant's
tail to show how big the
jewel was.

"Oh, no!" screamed Kali.
She was falling to Earth, and
so was everyone else. They
never made it to the bazaar
in heaven. And they never got
to buy the jewels that were
"about this big."

The
Magic
Eagle

Venezuela (Timotean Indians)

 Long ago the people of the Andes mountains believed in a god called Ches. One day Ches came down from the top of his mountain. He brought a gift to the chief of the mountain people. It was a statue of a golden eagle. It was more beautiful than anything the people had ever seen.

"This eagle is magic," Ches explained to the chief. "It will bring your people good luck. Take good care of it until the day I ask for it back."

"We will wait for your sign," said the chief.

The magic eagle did bring good luck to the mountain people. They always had food to eat, and they lived in peace. The eagle passed from one chief to the next, over many years. Still, there came no sign from Ches to return the eagle.

Then, for the first time, a young woman became the chief. She was kind and just, and everyone liked her. But she was not in good health. She became so sick that no doctor could make her well. The people painted themselves red and danced in a circle. They begged Ches to save their chief.

One morning the young chief called her helper and friend, Mistafa, into her room. "I had a dream last night," the chief told Mistafa. "Ches wants the magic eagle back now. It must be buried beside his temple. I am not strong enough to carry it to the top of the mountain. You, instead, must take it there."

"I would do anything to help you," said Mistafa. "But only a chief can find the way to the top of the mountain."

"Ches will help you," said the chief. "I am sure of that."

So Mistafa took the magic eagle and began her trip. The bird was very heavy.

Sometimes Mistafa was afraid she wouldn't make it. She often stopped to rest. Then she saw the temple of Ches ahead of her. Her feet felt light the rest of the way up the mountain.

Mistafa used a stone to dig a hole beside the temple. She placed the eagle in the hole and covered it with dirt. Then she lay down to rest beside this spot. She didn't mean to fall asleep, but she did.

When she woke up, it was morning. Mistafa looked around. "Am I in the same place?" she wondered. Beside her, instead of fresh dirt, was a large green bush with purple flowers.

Just then Mistafa heard a voice. "Take leaves from this bush back to your people," the voice said. "Make a strong tea, and be sure the chief drinks all of it."

Mistafa was sure this was the voice of Ches. She picked as many leaves as she could carry. Then she headed back down the mountain. She ran the whole way home.

Right away Mistafa made the tea for the chief. By now the chief was very weak. But Mistafa got her to drink every drop of the tea.

The next morning the chief sat up in bed. The day after that she began to walk. In a week's time the chief was well again.

The magic eagle had become a plant. The tea from its leaves made not only the chief well, but also many other people ever since.

A Strange Place to Visit

Vietnam

A young man left home to study in a big city. Every day, as he walked to school, he passed a big, old house that was falling apart. It looked as if no one had lived there for many years. However, there was a beautiful garden full of green plants, flowers, and fruit trees.

One day the student saw two young women running in the garden. They smiled at the student and threw flowers at him as he walked by.

The next day and the next, the same thing happened. The young man enjoyed hearing the women laugh. He loved it when they threw flowers at him.

"Will you have tea with me?" he asked them one day.

"I would love to," said the first woman.

"So would I," said the second woman.

"I'll stop by for you after school today," said the student.

He and the two women began having tea together every afternoon. The three of them wrote poems together and read each other what they wrote. They had a nice time. But the student fell behind in his school work.

"We always have tea at your place," said the first woman one day.

"We would like to throw a party for you in our garden," said the second woman.

"That would be lovely," said the student.

A lovely party it was. The night was warm, and the sweet smell of flowers filled the air. The garden was full of people. The people were all dressed as if they were from another time.

Not long after the party, the student got a letter from his parents. They were not happy about his school work suffering. They felt he might as well come home and get married. They had already found him a wife.

The student went home as his parents asked. "Of course I will marry the woman you chose for me," he said. "But, I beg you, can we put off the wedding for a little while? I would like to give school another try."

"Very well," said his parents.

But when the student got back to the city, he did not study. He went to see the two young women. Right away he could see that something was wrong with them.

"The weather is getting cold," said the first woman.

"We cannot live in cold weather," said the second woman.

"We will soon be gone," said the first woman.

"Is there anything I can do to help you?" asked the student.

"Nothing," said the second woman.

That night the air became very cold. The student was afraid of what might happen to his two friends. He went to visit his neighbor, an old man. He told him about the two young women at the old house.

"What are you talking about?" said the old man. "No one has lived in that house for over 20 years."

"Go there with me tomorrow," said the student. "I will show you."

The next day the student took the old man to the house. The two young women were not there. The garden was nothing but weeds.

"There was a big party here just a few weeks ago," said the student.

"What were the names of the people at that party?" asked the old man.

The student named everyone he could remember.

"How interesting!" said the old man. "Those are the names of the plants and flowers that grew here many years back. You have been living in a dream world, my friend."

That night the student dreamed about the two women. In his dream they spoke to him.

"We have had such a nice time with you," said the first woman.

"But life is short," said the second woman.

"One cannot play all his days away!" said the first woman.

"You must get back to your school work," said the second woman.

"Goodbye, goodbye," they both said.

The next day the student went back to the garden for one last visit. As he walked among the weeds he came upon two pairs of shoes. He remembered his friends wearing these shoes. As he picked them up, they turned into flowers, and their petals fell to the ground. In a moment, the student's hands were empty.

Talk

West Africa

It was the end of the growing season. A farmer went out to dig up potatoes. He pushed his shovel into the ground. Just then a potato said, "Well, look who's here. You didn't show up all season to clear out the weeds. Why come here now? Go away!"

The farmer looked over at his dog. "Did you say something?" he asked.

"It was the potato," said the dog. "Leave it alone!"

The farmer had never heard his dog talk. He didn't like the way she spoke to him. "Well, aren't you the smart one?" said the farmer. He reached for the palm tree to cut off a branch and hit the dog with it.

"Put that down!" said the palm tree.

The farmer started to throw down the branch. As he did, the branch said, "Be gentle!"

The farmer laid the branch on a stone. As he did, the stone said, "Take that off me!"

The farmer was afraid of all these talking things. He began to run. As he ran, he came upon a man on his way to go fishing. The man carried a fish trap on his head.

"What's the matter with you?" asked the man.

"My potato said, 'Go away!'" explained the farmer. "Then my dog said, 'Leave it alone!' When I got a branch to hit the dog with, the palm tree said, 'Put that down!' When I started to throw it down, the branch said, 'Be gentle!' When I laid the branch on a stone, the stone said, 'Take that off me!'"

"Did you take the branch off the stone?" asked the fish trap.

When the man heard his trap talk, he almost jumped out of his skin. He threw the trap off his head and ran off down the road with the farmer.

The two of them came upon a third man. This man was taking a bath in the river.

"What's the matter with you two?" asked the man in the river.

"When I tried to dig up a potato, it said, 'Go away!'" explained the farmer. "Then my dog said, 'Leave it alone!' When I tried to get a branch to hit the dog with, the palm tree said, 'Put that down!' When I started to throw the branch down, it said, 'Be gentle!' When I laid the branch on a stone, the stone said, 'Take that off me!'"

"And then my fish trap said, 'Did you take the branch off the stone?'" added the second man.

"What's the big deal?" asked the third man.

"If you heard such talk, you would run, too!" said the river.

The third man jumped out of the river when he heard it talk. He ran off down the road with the other two men.

When the three men reached the village, they went to see the chief. The chief sat on his special stool to hear the men tell their story. "Now, what happened?" asked the chief.

"When I tried to dig up a potato, it said, 'Go away!'" explained the farmer. "Then my dog said, 'Leave it alone!' When I tried to get a branch to hit the dog with, the palm tree said, 'Put that down!' When I started to throw the branch down, it said, 'Be gentle!' When I laid the branch on a stone, the stone said, 'Take that off me!'"

"And then my fish trap said, 'Did you take the branch off the stone?'" said the second man.

"And the river said, 'You would run, too!'" added the third man.

"Well, that's some story!" laughed the chief. "But I think you're all making a big fuss over nothing. Now go back to work, all of you!"

The three men left the village and went back to what they were doing.

The chief said, "Why do people tell such silly stories?"

"What's so silly about a talking potato?" said the chief's special stool. "Everything in the world has something to say."

The Mirror

Korea and Japan

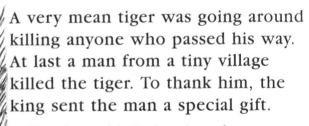

A very mean tiger was going around killing anyone who passed his way. At last a man from a tiny village killed the tiger. To thank him, the king sent the man a special gift.

"Look at this," the tiger hunter called to his wife. "What do you suppose it is?"

His wife took the thing in her hand. It was round and shiny and had a handle. Living in this village all her life, she had never seen anything like it. She held it by the handle.

"Why do you show me this?" she said to her husband. "I see the face of another woman. Have you taken a second wife? Get her out of here!"

The tiger hunter took the thing and held it up. "I do not see a woman's face," he said. "I see the face of a man. I have not taken a second wife. You have taken a second husband!"

"I have not!" shouted the woman. "When I look at this thing I see a woman. When you look at it you see a man. This must be magic."

The tiger hunter's mother came into the room. "What is going on here?" she asked.

"Take this thing in your hand," said the tiger hunter. "Tell us what you see."

"I see the face of an old woman," she said. "She has gray hair, and her face is full of lines. How did she get in here? This must be magic."

Then the tiger hunter's father came in to see what was going on. He looked into the magic thing. "I see my own father in old age," said the father. "How can this be? He has been gone for many years. This must be magic."

"The king's men brought me this gift," said the tiger hunter. "They just left. Let's catch up with them and ask them what it is."

The tiger hunter and his wife, mother, and father ran after the king's men. When they found them, the tiger hunter said, "Tell us, what is this thing? When my wife looks into it, she sees another woman. When I look into it, I see another man. When my mother looks into it, she sees an old woman. When my father looks into it, he sees his father in old age. Is this magic?"

The king's men laughed so hard they fell down. "Have you never seen a mirror?" one of them said. "When you look into a mirror, you see your own face!"

The tiger hunter looked into the mirror. "Well, how about that?" he said. "So this is what I look like!"

He passed the mirror to his wife. She looked into it and said, "I have a pretty face!"

The wife passed the mirror to the mother. She looked into it and said, "When did I get so old?"

She passed the mirror to the father. He looked into it and said, "I look just like my father."

"This is not magic," said the king's men.

"It's magic for anyone who has never seen a mirror," said the tiger hunter.

Then he and his wife, mother, and father ran back to the village. They showed everyone the mirror. Now everyone wanted one. So the tiger hunter went all the way to the city. He brought back mirrors for the whole village, so that everyone could have a little magic of their own.

Why the Sea Is Salty

Norway

Once there were two brothers. One was rich, and the other was poor. The poor brother was hungry, so he went to his rich brother to ask for food.

"I'll give you food if you do what I tell you," said the rich brother.

"I'll do anything," said the poor brother.

"Here is a ham," said the rich brother. He threw the meat at his poor brother. "Don't eat it. Find someone to buy it."

It was hard for the poor brother not to eat the ham. But he did as his rich brother asked. He carried the ham to the next town. The first person he met was an old man sitting at the edge of town.

"Do you know anyone who might want to buy a ham?" the poor brother asked.

"Ha!" said the old man. "Walk into the town. Go into the first inn you see. Everyone there will beg to buy your ham. Tell them you will sell them the ham for the little mill behind the door. You will see what I mean."

The poor brother walked into town. He went into the first inn he saw. Just as the old man said, everyone begged to buy the ham. And there, behind a door, was the mill. In no time at all, the poor brother sold his ham for the little mill.

As he walked back out of town, he stopped to talk with the old man. "What is so special about this mill?" asked the poor brother.

"That mill will grind out anything you ask it to," said the old man.

"Anything at all?" asked the poor brother.

"Anything," said the old man. "The trick is how to stop it." Then he whispered in the poor brother's ear how to stop the mill.

The poor brother went home to his wife. "What have you there?" she asked. "You were supposed to get some food. We can't eat a little mill."

"Grind out a nice dinner!" the poor brother told the mill.

In a wink, he and his wife had a fine meal in front of them.

When the rich brother came to visit, he saw what the mill could do. The poor brother had only to say what he wanted and the mill would grind it out.

"I want that mill," said the rich brother.

"It's not for sale," said the poor brother.

"Name your price," said the rich brother.

"Five hundred dollars!" said the poor brother.

"Sold!" said the rich brother.

"Just one thing," said the poor brother. "I must keep the mill for two more months. Then you may have it."

For the next two months, the poor brother ground out all the food he would need for years to come. Then he gave the mill to his rich brother. But he did not explain how to stop the mill.

The rich brother took the mill home. "Grind me some fish soup," he shouted.

The mill began to grind out fish soup, then more fish soup, then more. Before long, the rich brother's whole house filled up with fish soup.

"Stop!" shouted the rich brother. But the mill kept on grinding. Fish soup poured out into the road and all over town. The rich brother's neighbors were swimming in fish soup.

The rich brother grabbed the mill and made his way to the poor brother's house.

"Take this thing back!" he said.

The poor brother laughed. "I'll take it back for five hundred dollars more."

The rich brother gave him the mill and the money, no questions asked.

The poor brother was happy to have the mill back. He ground out a beautiful house for himself and his wife. He ground out gold and covered the house with sheets of it. He ground out fine rugs and tables and chairs and everything he could think of.

People from all over heard about the man who became rich from a mill. They came to see all the mill had done. One day, a ship's captain stopped by.

"Do you think that mill could grind out salt?" he asked.

"Of course," said the man who was no longer poor.

"I sail far away just to get salt," said the captain. "That mill could save me a lot of trips across the sea. How much do you want for it?"

"A million dollars," said the man. He didn't think the captain would pay such a high price.

"Sold!" said the captain. "I just tell the mill what to grind, and it will grind it, right?" And off he went with the mill. He never asked how to stop it.

The captain went back on board his ship. At once he said to the mill, "Grind me some salt!"

The mill began to grind out salt, then more salt, then more. Before long, the whole ship filled up with salt.

"Stop!" shouted the captain. But the mill kept on grinding. Nothing the captain did or said could stop the mill from grinding out salt. The ship became so heavy with salt that it sank into the sea.

To this day, that little mill sits at the bottom of the sea. It never stops grinding out salt. And that is why the sea is salty.

The Thunderbird

Native American—Winnebago

Long before ships sailed to America, giants lived among the people of the land. One of these giants was named Nasan. He was one hundred feet tall and very strong. But he was lonely. He wanted a wife.

One night Nasan looked up at the sky. He saw Evening Star Lady, shining bright and clear. All the people loved this star, for she was very beautiful. She helped them count their days and told them what the sun was doing. Nasan decided he wanted Evening Star Lady to be his wife.

So Nasan asked Needle Woman to make him wings. He tied the wings to his strong back and flew up into the sky. There he gave Evening Star Lady gifts of skins and beads. He asked her to come back with him. She said yes and flew to Earth on Nasan's back.

That night, when the people looked up at the sky, Evening Star Lady was not there. They missed her very much. Gone was the beautiful star that counted the days. The sun came and went without warning. The people begged the Great Spirit to get Evening Star Lady back into the sky.

The Great Spirit told Nasan to let her go. But Nasan loved her too much to give her up. He drew a magic circle all around his house. No one could get inside this circle.

The Great Spirit did not give up. He knew that ants lived in the ground under Nasan's house. He told the ants his plan to get Nasan out of the magic circle.

That night Nasan and Evening Star Lady heard voices under the floor. "There is a beautiful white deer about," the ants were saying. "The skin of this deer would make a fine robe."

"I must have it!" Evening Star Lady said to Nasan.

"I will get it for you," Nasan told her.

The next morning Nasan walked outside. He forgot all about the magic circle. He forgot that the Great Spirit wanted Evening Star Lady back in the sky.

As soon as Nasan left the magic circle, the Great Spirit caught him. They fought each other like no others have ever done. The fight went on for four days. At last Nasan crashed to the ground.

The Great Spirit sent Evening Star Lady back where she belonged. To this day, she shines in the night sky for everyone to see.

As for Nasan, the Great Spirit gave him a new name: Thunderbird. He flies around and around the sky, making storm clouds. Even now, the sound of thunder is the voice of the Thunderbird. And the lightning bolts that flash across the sky are the Thunderbird's wings, flying until the end of time.